Brand

Smart

by **Vince Rogers**

Vision Media Ventures
A subsidiary of Vince Rogers & Associates

1st Edition published by **Vision Media Ventures**

Copyright: © 2014 by **Vincent L. Rogers** *All rights reserved.*
ISBN: 978-1-304-76872-8

Vision Media Ventures
P.O. Box 77222, Atlanta, GA 30357-1222
United States of America

All images courtesy of **www.freedigitalphotos.net**

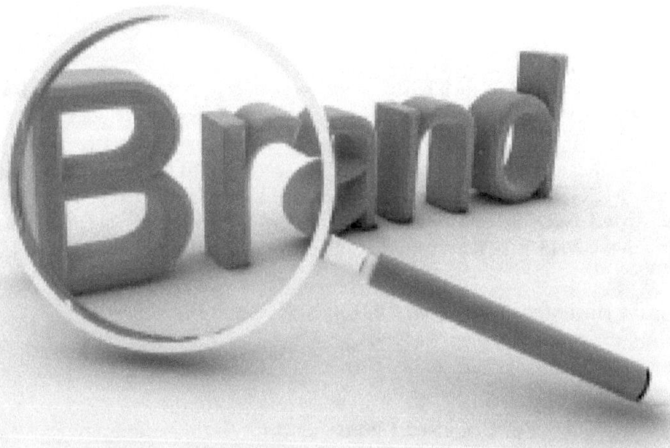
Brand

Vince Rogers  is an experienced resource manager and communications strategist. He is academically trained in economics, marketing, project management and professional communications. He is a graduate of the **Andrew Young School of Policy Studies** where he studied International and Urban Economics and the **J. Mack Robinson College of Business** where he studied Business Communications and Marketing. He possesses many years of successful experience in financial services and real estate management and marketing.

He is the **Principal Change Agent** at Vince Rogers & Associates www.vincerogers.biz

VINCE ROGERS
Resources Management
& Communications Consultants
& ASSOCIATES

He has been profiled in such business media outlets as **Atlanta Business RadioX** on the shows **High Velocity Radio** http://highvelocityradio.businessradiox.com/?p=1061 and **Write Here, Write Now** http://writeherewritenow.businessradiox.com/?powerpress_pinw=198-podcast which is cited as an essential resource in Appendix IV of the book **Publishing as a Marketing Strategy** (BookLogix Publishing Services, 2011 ISBN: 9781610051149) His article *Building Your Brand as a Consultant by Utilizing the "Keys to Success"* is featured as the †Cutting Edge Topic in the **2013 Pfeiffer Annual: Consulting** (John Wiley, 2012 ISBN: 978-1-1182-7379-1)

He is the Host of the *eHow.com "Business Success" Video Series* @ www.ehow.com/videos-on_12239455_business-success.html His video *"How to Develop a LinkedIn Relationship"* is a **2012 eHow.com Top-Performing Video**

He is the publisher of **Disguised Limits** @ http://disguisedlimits.blogspot.com which is **#2 in the Motivational category** @ Networked Blogs.com www.networkedblogs.com/topic/motivational

Disguised Limits
DISCOVER LIFE'S UNLIMITED OPPORTUNITIES!

"The Very Best of Disguised Limits" books are available to buy or download free @ www.lulu.com/product/16215088 & www.lulu.com/product/20371359

Greetings:

Your branding strategy is a living, breathing and perpetually evolving entity. Just like the activities of a real person, your branding efforts serve to build long lasting perceptions. The reputation that you build is based on people's opinions about your brand's appearance and personality and by how many people have been influenced by your branding efforts. Your branding strategy irreversibly shapes public perception and serves to form an enduring legacy.

The 30 concise but powerful articles that comprise *__Brand Smart__* will provide you with all of the essential knowledge needed to build a successful branding strategy. Within these pages you will find expert information that empowers you with basic knowledge, advanced concepts and innovative *"game-changing"* branding ideas. *__Brand Smart__* will provide you with the tools and resources needed to build a first-class personal brand. It will also help you to develop a professional branding strategy that will elevate your organization high above the competition.

I write a regular column on Personal Branding for Examiner.com that provides readers with expert information on building a strong professional identity. I have published numerous articles as an EzineArticles.com Expert Author on the subjects of: *Success; Entrepreneurialism; Personal Finance; Public Relations; Productivity; Marketing; Branding; Careers; Presentations; Business* and *Consulting.* Through my work as the **Principal Change Agent @ Vince Rogers & Associates www.vincerogers.biz,** I have created two unique sets of concepts that I use to help businesses, non-profits and high achieving individuals to formulate winning "Success Plans" for reaching their desired destinations - the *"Six Keys to Success"* and the *"Big Fundamentals of Success Planning".* All of these ideas are incorporated into the dynamic articles found in this indispensable volume on the subject of personal and professional branding.

After reading *__Brand Smart__* you will gain a new understanding of the subject of branding. You will learn that a branding strategy consists of more than having a nice logo and business cards. These things are important, but they represent only one aspect of your successful branding strategy. The information found in *__Brand Smart__* will empower you with the basic knowledge that you need to build your brand, the advanced ideas that you need to gain a dominant brand presence and innovative concepts that will help you to rise above even the sharpest competition.

Continued Success,

Branding Expert - Vince Rogers

Table of Contents

Smart

Protect Your Good Name

by **Vince Rogers**

William Shakespeare is considered to be the greatest arbiter of Western Literature to have ever lived. In his masterpiece of treachery and envy, "Othello," he may have also delivered the most useful idiom to remember while continuously building your personal brand. In Act 3, Scene 3, of the play, the villainous Iago delivers a soliloquy that summarizes the essence of building your brand and managing your reputation:

"Good name in man and woman, dear my lord,

Is the immediate jewel of their souls.

Who steals my purse steals trash; 'tis something, nothing;

'Twas mine, 'tis his, and has been slave to thousands;

But he that filches from me my good name

Robs me of that which not enriches him,

And makes me poor indeed."

Personally, I first learned these powerful words from my beloved grandmother many years ago. She tried to instill this valuable lesson in me time and time again. Grandma was a great proponent of strategic branding and reputation management long before these terms were in vogue. She just prescribed these maxims under the general heading of lessons you need to learn in order to be regarded as a good person.

Nowadays numerous books, seminars, DVD and CD programs are available to purchase on the topics of personal branding, brand management reputation management and various nuances and augmentations of these themes. Many of these products have information that is vital and if applied can make a great deal of impact in your life. As you continue to follow this column, I will share many such valuable tools and resources that I have developed or researched especially for you. However, I am convinced that many of the most essential, powerful and easily implementable keys to building your brand are the things you learned just as I did as a child.

There are six keys to success that are essential to building a winning success plan. While these attributes are the key to implementing your overall success strategy, they are also integral to building your personal brand as well. These six keys to success have been adapted to meet the complex demands of modern day enterprise building.

However, you should realize very quickly that they are based on simple lessons that we've all learned over the years. Integrity in dealing with people, common sense in matters of good judgment and exercising good stewardship over the resources at your disposal are the essential requirements for successful personal branding.

1. Information: Become known as a trustworthy subject matter expert in your field.
2. Image: Go out into the world every day and look, sound and act the way you want to be treated.
3. Initiative: Always act on the basis of sound planning and good research, which leads to the pursuit of effective strategy.

4. **Confidence:** Through dedicating yourself to winning small victories, you will be emboldened with the confidence that you've done your best; this will be the basis of the momentum that propels you to success.

5. **Capital:** The greatest source of future revenue and profits for your business will be determined by the purchasing and cost decisions you make today.

6. **Contacts:** You must assemble a winning team. You alone will never possess all of the skills and abilities required for perfection, nor will you ever be able to earn every certification or degree needed to answer every question.

In summary: You and you alone are responsible for controlling the quality of your brand. The image you present and the information you transfer to the public are signs of your dedication to quality and the soundness of your ideas. Many vital aspects contribute to successfully building a powerful personal brand.

In most instances, if we would heed the vital life lessons we learned from our parents, grandparents and even the sage wisdom from the tales written by the Bard of Avon, we would be just fine. The answers we seek most often come when we remember to keep it simple, keep it honest and keep it consistent.

Career Branding Using LinkedIn
by **Vince Rogers**

In the brave new world of *"social networking"* websites, it can be difficult to resist the urge to mix business with pleasure. We often hear of anecdotal references to people, especially young people in the early stages of building a career having negative outcomes because of decision makers "Googling" their FaceBook pages and reading their random Twitter "Tweets". Potential bosses and co-workers are allowed to bear witness to them engaging in various youthful acts of indiscriminate activities that can hinder their career and professional mobility. Although tailoring the privacy settings of your account should suffice to prevent these intrusions into your online realm, the more purely social sites are not really the proper setting to build your professional brand in the first place - unless of course you are a burgeoning club promoter, top bikini model or stand-up comic.

FaceBook is very popular with young professionals. It provides access to a wide array of fun applications, games and social events. It can also be used as a tool to help brand yourself. You may do this by posting relevant content to your page that can be read by your "friends".

Twitter is another widely popular portal to the world of social networking. It allows you to communicate succinct messages to your "followers". The site also allows you to follow important contacts. You can even send *targeted messages* to key people.

However, for the most part both of these sites give users access to a wide array of purely fun applications. Because the goal is primarily to have fun, most people have a hard time presenting a cohesive professional image using these sites. Instead, many people who attempt to use these sites to help build their personal brand, can't resist engaging in the less professional offerings that drive the success of social networking sites. Ultimately, they end up with pages consisting of a mix of some pertinent information peppered with an assortment of cool, but potentially damaging pictures, random quasi-humorous "tweets" and other non essential content.

When it comes to career and professional branding and positioning, *LinkedIn* **www.linkedin.com** is a more relevant social networking tool. It can be most adequately utilized to establish a well conceived, powerful and consistent personal branding strategy on the World Wide Web. LinkedIn allows you to be proactive with your branding strategy, rather than hoping that the right people see your posts on the other social sites and that after reading the information they somehow "get" you.

Of course with any successful branding strategy, you must take the time to conceive and execute a plan that addresses your desired outcome. This strategy should achieve the dual goal of positioning you as an expert and networking with the people who you want to make aware of your expertise. There are essentially **3 Keys to Creating a Successful Branding Strategy on LinkedIn:**

1) Create a Powerful *Profile* page.

2) Strategically Build Your Network of *Contacts*

3) Join the Right *Groups*.

These three topics will be covered in more depth in future articles.

In the mean time, the keys to personal branding that you will need as you start to use LinkedIn are the same skills you will need as you pursue any personal branding strategy. As you build your profile on LinkedIn, remember that you are attempting to position yourself as a trustworthy subject matter expert in your field. Then as you pursue the task of building your contacts, keep in mind that you must assemble a winning team in order to achieve long-term career and professional success. To further acquaint yourself with the keys to building a powerful personal brand, please read the article: **Protect Your Good Name**.

See You on the Radio:

Personal Branding Using Internet Talk Radio

by Vince Rogers

The question of the day when it comes to branding, promoting and marketing products and services is how can I use "new media" effectively? The catch-all phrase "new media" refers to the advent of technological advancements in computers, communications technology and computer-enabled communications devices. Most importantly, the internet has made it possible to reach potential customers in ways that were unimaginable just a few years ago. It is clear that using these new platforms effectively is essential to building, promoting and maintaining your brand. The most important question to consider then is what "new media" vehicle can I use to reach the customers I need to reach?

Atlanta Business RadioX http://atlantabusinessradiox.com
offers a very cost-effective solution to this problem that gives marketers a considerable "Bang for the Buck". The "station" enables marketers to produce talk shows and informational programs that are uniquely targeted to specific audiences. These programs are broadcast live over the internet to their regular listeners. However, the greatest benefit is to be gained by using the "podcasts" of the programs to reach your network of clients and potential prospects in your targeted branding efforts.

At the helm of Atlanta Business RadioX is veteran producer Lee Kantor. According to Kantor, "People do business with people they know. And what's a better way to get to know someone than by interviewing them on your own internet radio talk show?" That's right, for a nominal investment you can host your own radio show, create tailored content to suit your audience, and distribute that content to a wide audience of regular listeners of the station and to your own targeted audience as well.

There are many other reciprocal benefits and brand building opportunities for the hosts as well as guests appearing on the shows such as:

- By hosting your own radio show you can invite your best prospects to be a guest on your show.
- By appearing as a guest you can use your appearance to position yourself as an expert in your field.
- You can appear as a guest or host a show to meet other thought leaders in your industry.
- You can take advantage of advertising and sponsorship opportunities utilizing their broad lineup of shows.

I can personally attest to the effectiveness of Atlanta Business RadioX as a branding tool. I appeared as a guest on one of their flagship shows, **High Velocity Radio http://highvelocityradio.businessradiox.com** The show is hosted by veteran marketing and media experts Stone Payton and Todd Schick. The High Velocity Radio show's mission is *"Celebrating Top Performers Producing Better Results In Less*

Time". The free flowing, engaging yet highly informative format of the show allowed me to confidently present my message to my target audience in a succinct, powerful and effective way.

To find out more information about how you can host your own show or appear as a guest on one of the existing shows on **Atlanta Business RadioX** please contact Lee Kantor directly at **404-786-3765** or email him at **lee@businessradiox.com**

Using Professional Photography to Build Your Brand
by **Vince Rogers**

There is an old adage that says *"A picture is worth a thousand words."* To state it another way, a bad picture makes zero impact. These days it may be possible to take good pictures and create effective headshots yourself. However, you may want to consider using a professional photographer to gain the maximum impact for your brand.

Cost effective and easy to use digital cameras have given the masses access to tools that were once only accessible to professionals. While technology has somewhat leveled the playing field, the techniques employed by a professional photographer may be what your branding efforts really require. The strategic usage of the right photo of you receiving a big award, making an important public appearance or achieving a significant career milestone can pay big dividends. You may not want to trust the responsibility of capturing that big moment to your significant other or next door neighbor.

According to Atlanta native and noted celebrity photographer Quinn Hood of Global Images, *"Celebrities and high profile people continue to utilize professional photographers because of the expertise they bring in the way of composition, lighting and other key technical aspects of taking a great photo."* Hood has photographed such celebrities as U2 front man Bono, baseball legend Hank Aaron, pioneering music producer Dallas Austin and over the years has built a vital relationship with movie star Chris Tucker. The world famous comedian has found his services so essential to building his brand that he has flown him to Africa on several occasions to capture his many photo ops with foreign dignitaries and world leaders.

Even though a photo is just a still image, it should tell a great story. The background, foreground, subject placement and framing of a photo are the elements of a shoot that good professional photographers are paid to combine to make a winning photograph. According to Hood, *"The subject is just one element of a good shot, my job is to make the subject into a verb – then the person looking at it turns it into a complete sentence."* The story that sentence tells to your audience will determine how they will remember your brand.

To reach **Quinn Hood Global Images** call **404-895-1394** or by e-mail @ **ghood@bellsouth.net**

The Final Four: Health; Wealth; Fame; and Family
by **Vince Rogers**

In the Bible, there are numerous useful prescriptions for living a meaningful life. Most of them are also relevant in the areas of success planning and personal branding. One of, if not the most important of these Biblical maxims can be found in the Book of Proverbs. Proverbs 20:10 states that *"...Even a child is known by his actions, by whether his conduct is pure and right...."* Simply stated, a person shall be known by what they do with the bountiful gifts and talents that they have possessed since they were a child.

However, many of us remain acutely focused on the superficial goals of a child, instead of the loftier pursuits of our higher selves. We set a goal to become thin instead of becoming healthy, in order to change our childhood perception of being the fat kid. We set a goal to earn extreme financial wealth because we grew up "poor" of worldly possessions, even if we grew up in a family that enjoyed vast moral and spiritual abundance. Most importantly, we set a goal to achieve fame based on hollow achievements, rather than being renowned because of a well earned reputation for excellence.

Fame and Wealth are the most outwardly visible manifestations of success. Yet celebrity and fortune can be achieved just as easily by a drug dealer as it can be by a heart surgeon. Achieving your place of distinction in the world by doing things the right way will enable you to truly enjoy the prosperity that it brings. Doing things the right way means doing things in a way that allows you to maintain your health and sanity as well as your family and friendships.

The importance of balancing your quest for fame and fortune with good physical and mental health habits, along with nurturing your family and friendships is inestimable. Focusing on these things in turn will also contribute greatly to the pursuit of the goals that will lead you to fame and fortune. It is inconceivable that you can achieve the success you desire weighed down by physical illness and besieged by emotional anxiety. Conversely, a person who neglects his friendships and family is unlikely to have success at building the necessary network that will help them to achieve the fame and wealth that they so greatly desire.

Health; Wealth; Fame; and Family are the four pillars of living a successful and balanced life. Good health and strong family alone are the essential measures of a live well lived. Yet many people strive to leave some legacy of their life's work as well. Achieving a measure of material wealth and a level of high esteem associated with your name can also benefit your family. Acquiring these things gives you and your loved one's a better chance of living a long healthy life filled with joy and abundance.

Capital Ideas - Optimizing Purchase and Cost Decisions
by **Vince Rogers**

It has been said that the number one reason for business failure is under-capitalization. Yet stories abound of legendary business successes that lacked adequate resources in their formative stages. Conversely, well capitalized businesses often fail miserably. What ultimately proves to be the key reason for the success of most businesses is passionate entrepreneurial leadership and visionary strategic planning.

Yet when it comes to business success, money certainly matters. However, in many cases it isn't how much cash you have access to that determines viable cash flow. More importantly, spending the cash that you have efficiently has the greater impact on long-term business success or failure. The greatest source of future revenue and profits for your business will be determined by the purchasing and cost decisions you make today.

In fact, many well capitalized businesses tend to purchase things outright with their cash rather than pursue other more optimal ways of acquiring the things they need. Some well capitalized businesses often tend to try to find a reason to buy everything; instead of finding a way to avoid buying anything. In many instances, having the money to buy something often creates the false perception that the company can "afford" acquisitions that are often ill-advised or more appropriate at a later date. Should the business ultimately fail, they are then stuck with a lot of illiquid assets on their balance sheet and defaulted loans or angry investors.

It is important that you look at each cost and purchase decision you make as a link in your "value-chain". In other words, does the associated cost and terms of making this acquisition add long term value to my business? Does making this expenditure enable me to offer a higher quality product or service to my customer? Making purchasing and cost decisions in this way also puts you in the habit of thinking about your business strategically at all times.

Making good purchase decisions doesn't always mean getting the lowest price. Spending a few dollars more for a higher quality product or with a better established supplier can often lead to more satisfied customers, quicker delivery times and even gaining referral business from the supplier. Also, it may be possible through negotiation to convert a prospective vendor into a business partner instead. Sometimes this can be done without having to pay anything.

For instance, it may be worth more to the local sandwich shop to cater your roundtable meeting of local Executives for free or reduced costs in order to market their business to the purchasing managers and decision-makers attending the conference. You should always be looking to cut deals that benefit your bottom line, rather than being a free spender of your company's scarce resources. Other ways to cut costs may be to share office space with strategic companies, bartering your goods and services in exchange for the things you need and buying used office equipment and furniture rather than buying these things new.

It may not always be easy to weigh every factor of each individual purchase. However, failing to examine the key factors of buying may prove to be disastrous. As the fictional character Gordon Gekko stated in "Wall Street", the classic Hollywood film *"A fool and his money are lucky enough to get together in the first place."* As difficult as it is to find the money to start and grow a successful business, surely the last thing you want to do is make the avoidable cost and purchasing decisions that often lead to ultimate business failure.

From Blog to Book: The Easy Road to "Infopreneurship"
by **Vince Rogers**

It is often said that *content is king* when it comes to building an online presence for your brand. One of the most cost effective and high impact ways to generate and distribute the high quality content that you produce is through publishing a blog. As a subject matter expert in your field, it should not be very difficult to regularly produce high-quality content in order to generate a very informative, well followed blog. The content that you generate and a place to publish it are all that you need to get started on the easy road to "Infopreneurship".

If you are not already blogging, the process for getting started is fairly simple. There are quite a few popular *blog publishing services* that can be used to create your own high quality blog. Some of the more popular outlets are **TypePad**, **Blogger** (which is owned by**Google.com**) and **WordPress**. You can easily determine which of these (or the many other) sites will fit your particular needs. The most common approach to making that decision is through either utilizing trial and error, researching comparisons online or by soliciting referrals from other bloggers.

Personally, I use the Blogger platform to publish my highly popular blog **Disguised Limits**(**www.disguisedlimits.blogspot.com**) Disguised Limits provides readers with useful articles and special updates about local networking opportunities, offers and discounts, business and sales leads, plus an abundance of other useful business and life enhancing information. When I started to blog, going with the service that had the word blog in the name just made sense to me. You might choose to go with a more scientific approach.

Disguised Limits is the #2 blog in the Opportunities category on **NetwokedBlogs.com**. NetworkedBlogs.com is a blog directory that is maintained by **Facebook.com**. Blog directories are services that list popular blogs, much like an on-line index or card catalog to assist blog followers. Using blog directories enables your blog to gain greater exposure to a wider audience than just relying on being followed by random users of your chosen blog publishing service.

There are also local blogging professionals that can provide you with their expertise to help you build your dynamic blog-based branding machine. Atlanta social media maven **Judi Knight** of **New Tricks** (**www.newtricks.me**) is one of the most sought after and well respected website and blog design experts around town. Knight is a passionate proponent of using social media along with blogging to empower entrepreneurs to *"....capture their "essence" in order to build their brand and grow their businesses...."*

The most well designed and highly informative blog on the internet is nothing without followers. I cannot emphasize strongly enough that the best way to gain a large captive audience of loyal followers is by regularly generating high quality content that is relevant to your target audience. To promote this content and increase their blog's following; most bloggers utilize their existing networks on the most popular social media platforms

Twitter, FaceBook, LinkedIn etc. Some other useful tips to growing your blog's readership and fan base are to:

1) Use the blog traffic analytics provided by your blog publishing service to determine the readership patterns of your existing followers.

2) Make widgets or gadgets (apps that link your blog to other websites) available for readers to place on their social media pages, personal websites and personal blogs.

3) Interact with your blog followers by being responsive to their comments on your blog.

4) Follow as many other blogs as you can and regularly interact with other bloggers.

Now that you're the publisher of a successful blog with an avid following, what's next? You are the owner of your blog content and therefore free to publish your articles in any other online and print publications. For most bloggers utilizing their blog to grow their business is more than enough payoff for their effort and ingenuity. However, some savvy bloggers may want to take it a step further by using their blog content to enter the realm of information marketing.

Information marketing is the business of selling Books, e-Books, CDs, DVDs, Webinars Podcasts, etc. to consumers seeking essential knowledge that they can use to enhance their business or professional lives. The most fundamental information products are "inspirational""motivational" "self-help" or "how-to" books. Turning your blog content into a book provides you with the perfect opportunity to enter the domain of legendary

"Infopreneurs" such as Robert Kyosaki, Jim Rohn, Les Brown and Atlanta resident Dennis Kimbro.

The traditional route to getting a book publishing deal is one that you might consider. However, self publishing is the easiest route to bringing your book and or e-book to the public. As with the process of publishing your blog, several easy to use print-on-demand, self publishing sites exist on the internet. Some of the notable names in the game are **Lulu**, **AuthorHouse**, **xLibris** and **iUniverse**. These sites provide users with easy to use tools that allow authors to download simple text documents and images from their own computers to create actual hardcover or paperback books. Within a matter of minutes, you can produce a bookstore quality publication or e-Book that customers can purchase or download from their own computer.

I recently made the great leap into the information marketing space by turning my own blog into a book. "**The Very Best of Disguised Limits**" book is now available to buy or download free at **www.lulu.com** To market and promote your book; you will utilize many of the same tools that are used to market and promote your blog. The book has allowed me to create new business opportunities, expand my number of blog followers and make a few dollars from selling the book as well. The positive response to the book has been more than I ever expected. By following the steps I have outlined, I am sure that in no time flat you can also make the successful conversion from mere mortal blogger to successful Infopreneur "rock star" as well.

Building Your "Standout" Brand as a Consultant

by **Vince Rogers**

"I am a <u>consultant</u>." This declaration is probably heard more these days than the answer to the question "What is your name?" More than at any other time in history, this economy has prompted well educated highly skilled professionals to seek to earn a living by plying their trade without working for an employer. So how does the "standout" consultant rise above the masses of tenderfoot claimants who are just temporarily between jobs? Conversely, how can bright new consultants convince prospective clients that they are really tuned-in and not just singing the same old song?

The consulting trend is especially evident in a city like Atlanta. According to the Georgia Department of Labor, as of October 2011, the Metro Atlanta unemployment rate stood at 10.3%. That is more than a point above the national average. Yet many of these unemployed people are well trained and highly qualified. More importantly, the need for their skills has not disappeared. Most of these people were simply "laid off" in order for the company to cut the costs of salaries and benefits. Now these companies are challenged to continue to increase productivity with less manpower and faced with diminished brainpower.

Many of these displaced workers were key management and executive level employees. Because of their high salaries and the fact that there are fewer openings for top-level positions, they may have limited success finding a new job at the same level.

In order to earn a living, out of necessity these former long-time employees are now faced with the daunting task of becoming first time entrepreneurs.

Given the economic trends concerning workforce expansion and economic productivity, hiring consultants as opposed to full-time employees is becoming the rule rather than the exception. Translation: This isn't your grandmother's workforce. Progressively more opportunities to become a consultant may become available in the future than permanent full-time jobs created. According to Atlanta technology and publishing consultant **Leo Tucker**, author of the book ***Free Agent Executive*** *"Contractors or consultants are at the forefront of a revolution in the workforce."*

So what does it take to gain a foothold as a consultant in this current environment? Essentially all consultants have to do 3 things to succeed:

1) Define your area of expertise

2) Find Clients

3) Deliver a quality product

Numbers 1 and 3 will be determined by the experiences and abilities that you have acquired throughout your career. Number 2 will be a function of your efforts to effectively build and promote your brand in order to stand out from the competition.

When you walk into your local Home Depot in search of a new hammer, you assume the hammer is a good one because of the quality you expect from the Home Depot brand. To gain this same level of confidence from your prospective clients will require you to create the perception that your generic skills are of a higher quality than the identical skills presented by the next guy. This seems like it could be a daunting task. However, by employing a few strategies you can manage to stand out from the crowd.

As a reminder, there are 3 **Branding Fundamentals** that should always guide your **Branding Strategy**:

1) Build your Brand **Identity**

2) Maintain your Brand **Consistency**

3) Focus your Branding **Outreach**

The image you present through your marketing materials (business cards, correspondence, website, etc.) is very important. The information this *"identity package"* transfers to the public are the first signs of your dedication to quality. What these materials communicate will be the first sign that the potential client will receive as to the soundness of your thinking. You must make sure that these simple things create a lasting impression, which will help potential clients remember you instead of the other guy.

In this day and age you must build and manage a quality online reputation. There are a number of well known platforms available for establishing an online presence. However, most business people drop the ball when it comes to monitoring and managing their internet presence. The analytic tools of your various pages and blogs should be evaluated regularly to make sure you are consistently reaching your target market. Using online tools and social media better than the next guy will definitely give you a leg up on the competition.

Another vital yet overlooked key to successful branding is building and managing the right relationships. Who you associate with and are associated with can make more of a lasting impression than you ever could by attempting to make your own unassisted introduction to certain prospects. A referral from someone your client already knows and respects can be the key to opening the door to new business. Sometimes, it really does come down to who you know.

In summary, to attract customers as a consultant in this competitive environment you will have to stand out from the competition. Once you determine your area of specialization and determine the niche market that you will service, finding clients will be your greatest challenge. To be successful at building your business, you will have to build a brand that stands out from the competition. The keys to successfully leveraging that brand will be determined by maintaining the consistency of the brand and continuously engaging your target market.

"Re-Branding" Yourself When Facing Adversity
by **Vince Rogers**

You graduate from a historic and prestigious university. You land your dream job in the glamorous entertainment industry. You work directly with a music legend and famous celebrities. You are regarded in your profession as a highly talented and extremely energetic "*go-getter*". You become a Vice-President at one of the most iconic brand names in the entertainment industry. You are regarded as a real "*Big Deal*". You have it all.

You are diagnosed with Multiple Sclerosis (*MS*) at the age of 22. For years you manage to hide the debilitating limitations the condition imposes on you. Nevertheless, you devote 15 years to building an identity that is synonymous with confidence, competence and consistency. You accomplish all of this under the most challenging circumstances. But ultimately, the pressures of the fast paced, stressful world of the entertainment industry become too much to manage. This eventually leads to you being laid off from a job that has been your identity for more than a decade. You've lost it all. Now what?

*Six years ago, Atlanta based **Personal Brand Strategy** coach **Kelly Green** was faced with this exact dilemma. The simultaneous challenges of managing her serious health condition and the loss of her high-status career seriously shook the core of her identity. She affirms that*

"When I got laid off, I was hurt, angry and embarrassed, but most of all I had no idea what I was going to do next!"

After no small amount of soul searching, she decided for the first time in her life to put a priority on her own personal well being. This was not easy for someone who was used to putting their career first. As she puts it, "*My ego wanted to continue living the lifestyle I had been living for 15 years, but deep down I knew that I needed a mental and physical break from it all.*"

This realization highlights the first stage of what "**Coach Kelly**" characterizes as the process of "**Personal Re-Branding**" Many people are currently facing the process of repositioning their lives after facing serious adversities. Home foreclosure, job loss, severe illness and other major challenges can send a person's life into a tailspin. Not only can such life altering adversities affect how the world sees your personal brand identity, but they can deeply alter your personal self-image as well. Kelly believes that the first question you have to ask yourself in this process of personal "re-branding" is

"What do I want to do with my life now and how does my new situation affect that?"

She realized that if she was going to continue pursuing her dreams, she would first have to address her health situation. During this process she met with a Holistic Nutrition Coach while still residing in New York City. Not only was this encounter beneficial to her health, it also helped her identify the path she should take towards "*re-branding*" herself professionally. Luckily for us, she also decided to relocate to Atlanta to pursue what she describes as a "*better quality of life*".

Based on her experiences with wellness professionals, Kelly went on to become a **Certified Wellness Coach** herself. However in an "*Aha Moment*" she ascertained that her client's needs went beyond their emotional and physical wellness. She realized that they also needed help "*developing and clarifying their Brand*". Her years of experience in Marketing and her passion for helping people motivated her to combine these abilities to also become a *Personal Branding* **Strategist**.

The marketing of entertainers had been her job function in the fast-paced music industry. However, she realized that essentially her true passion was helping people realize their full potential. As she states it, she identified that there were other "*People just like me who needed to "re-brand" and needed to build a new identity.*"

Identifying your true passion and unique skills are essential to the "*re-branding*" process. This is true whether you find yourself facing the best of life's good fortune or the hardest of life's bad times. Some other key steps to follow in this process that Green has identified are:

- Position yourself as an expert regarding what you are passionate about.
- Identify a targeted niche population that needs your unique skills.
- Create a profile of an ideal client that needs your services. (Be Specific)
- Understand your **Unique Selling Proposition (USP)** that appeals to your ideal client.

Kelly emphasizes that understanding your *Unique Selling Proposition (USP)* is the key to understanding how to convert your passion into an actual income generating enterprise. Having faced great adversity herself enabled Green to embrace one of the most essential components to developing your *USP*. You must be able to

"....Speak to a potential client's "Pain Point" and demonstrate that you are uniquely qualified to solve their problem...."

An organization's "*Pain Point*" is defined as an area in which they are having trouble fulfilling a consumer's need. Green believes that her ability to empathize with people who are searching to establish or re-establish their identity is one of the keys to her success. "*I've seen what it's like when you don't understand your brand and how things open up when you do*" she says.

This process of "*re-branding*" has value not just for Green's customers who are mostly entrepreneurs and "*solo-service*" professionals. Developing your Personal Brand and identifying your *USP* can be useful for job seekers, career changers and even for people making a decision about academic pursuits. This is especially true when facing adversity.

Green firmly believes that you "*Don't be afraid to take the first steps no matter what the outcome will be.*" This process can be a totally individual effort, or it may require that you seek the guidance of a mentor or **Branding Coach**. In any event, Kelly believes that

"In order to communicate your value to other people, you have to know and understand your value first."

To learn more about Kelly Green please visit **www.insiderbrandingsecrets.com** or contact her at **kelly@insiderbrandingsecrets.com**

Branding Fundamentals: The Golden Rules of Personal Branding by **Vince Rogers**

Your branding strategy should be viewed as a living, breathing and perpetually evolving entity. Just as with the actions of an actual person, your branding efforts will build a lasting reputation. This reputation is based on people's perception of your brand's appearance, its personality and by how many people have been influenced by your efforts. Your branding strategy irreversibly shapes your public perception, professional reputation and enduring legacy.

Your branding strategy consists of more than just creating a nice logo and printing up some business cards. Although these things are important, they represent only one aspect of your successful branding strategy. Just like an Olympic athlete who strives to stand on the winner's podium, *mastering the fundamentals* is the key to "*Going for the Gold*". Also like an "Olympian", building a successful branding strategy is governed by adhering to the principles of the *I.O.C.* – **Identity; Outreach and Consistency.**

There are **3** essential *Branding Fundamentals* that make up the **Golden Rules of Personal Branding**:

1) Building Your Brand Identity

2) Focusing Your Brand Outreach

3) Maintaining Your Brand Consistency

The Brand Identity Package

Your **Brand Identity Package** consists of the tools that you will use to present your brand to the world. The basic components of your brand identity package are a *logo, tagline, business card and letterhead.* In addition to these basic components, most companies will also need a *website or blog and a brochure.* In many instances, the first time that someone receives your business card, letterhead and brochure or views your website and blog; they will make a first and final decision about who you are and what value you bring to the table.

Most people give the creation of their logo primary emphasis when formulating their identity package. Although often neglected, you should give the formulation of your tagline some very serious thought as well. Your tagline serves as a succinct but permanent **Elevator Pitch**. A powerful tagline should communicate your *Unique Selling Proposition (USP)* creatively, but clearly. In other words, it should explain in one sentence what it is that you do and what value you bring to the table.

Reaching Your Target Audience

You've invested a lot of time, money, effort and creativity into creating your brand identity. Now you want people to see what you've done. You really want to impress people with your big title, cool logo and witty tagline. Therefore, you should just give out all of your business cards to every pretty girl you meet at the bar and every old high school friend you run into at the reunion - right? Wrong.

The most effective way to succeed at building your brand is to determine your specific **Target Audience**. The first step to deciding on your Target Audience is to create a profile of your **Ideal Customer**. Once you have done this, you should try as much as possible to reach those people and only those people with your message. This will be the key to success of your well focused brand outreach strategy.

Always Be Consistently Consistent

It has been said that the only thing constant in life is change. On the other hand, it is also fairly clear that most people don't really like change. It is an absolute fact that the worst thing you can do when trying to build your brand is to keep changing the message. You should use the same images and value propositions consistently across all marketing channels.

Channels overlap frequently in today's complex marketing environment. The tagline on your business card can't communicate that you're the "low cost leader", but the tagline on your website says something different. Whether it's colors, graphics or taglines; constantly changing the elements of you brand identity leads to confusion. Confusion leads to uncertainty - uncertainty leads to risk. Ultimately, this perception of risk will lead to your prospects choosing the competition.

Some factors that you should consider in order to insure your brand consistency are to:

1) Use the Same Graphics Elements Across All Mediums

2) Formulate a Core Message and Stick With It

3) Always Communicate Your *Unique Selling Proposition*

4) Separate Business from Personal When Using Social Media

You should adapt your message to changing conditions if the essential elements of your branding strategy actually change. However, you should avoid making changes in order to chase trends or just to suit a single prospective client. Instead, when "going for the gold" you should always remember to adhere to the rules of the *I.O.C.* and stick to the fundamentals by playing by the "golden rules". Build a unique brand **Identity,** focus your brand's **Outreach** and maintain your brand's **Consistency.**

Using Expert Videos to Build Your Personal Brand

by **Vince Rogers**

You've reached the pinnacle of your profession. Now you want to continue building your brand by sharing your expertise on the "big screen". Okay maybe we'll start with computer monitors and "smartphones" and work our way up to the big screen later. Lights; Cameras; Action! – you're ready to make a professionally produced expert video.

I was recently called upon to do just that, by filming a "Business Success" video series for eHow.com. Although the experience was personally and professionally rewarding, it was certainly no "walk in the park". Many elements go into making a high quality video that presents your brand in the best light. You must select the right topic for your audience, refine your content for effective presentation and also choose the right location in order to produce a high quality finished product. Most importantly, you must work with a highly experienced, technically proficient, and creatively perceptive filmmaker.

The filmmaker for my project certainly fit the bill. Atlanta filmmaker Edward Castner has 20+ years of experience in all aspects of film production camera work and film editing. Some of his previous projects include work for the Discovery Channel, National Geographic Channel, BBC ITN and the National Gallery of Art. He also spent three weeks in New Orleans covering the aftermath of Hurricane Katrina. Even before the actual video shoot took place, Ed was instrumental in advising me to create visual aids that would enhance my oral presentation. According to Ed, "Most people fail to realize how important strong visuals are to the effectiveness of a good video."

The actual "filmic" elements of the video are not the only details you must pay attention to. When making an "expert" video, your appearance and presentation are still the most essential elements. You should pay close attention to the following personal details:

- **Wear attire that is well suited to your level of expertise**
- **Make sure that your voice and language are tailored to your audience**
- **Limit the length of your video to the minimum time needed to explain the topic**
- **Try to be aware of your facial expressions, posture and body language**

Even with Ed's patience and professionalism, I still found the experience of making my first videos much harder than I anticipated. Getting used to the camera as your only audience is a challenge to say the least. Getting used to the penetrating hot lights burning right through you is another matter altogether. It would have been almost impossible to manage this process without the help of a seasoned professional filmmaker. If you would like to contact Ed Castner to capture your brand and expertise on film you may contact him at **www.edcastner.com/contact**

To view the finished product of our video shoot visit

http://www.ehow.com/videos-on_12239455_business-success.html

How to Develop a Strong LinkedIn Relationship
by **Vince Rogers**

Developing strong relationships on **LinkedIn** can be very important to career and business success. LinkedIn has over 150 million registered users and is still growing. It is the most powerful *professional networking* site on the internet.

"Social Networking" sites allow users to mix business with pleasure. LinkedIn is a purely *Professional Networking* site. Therefore the ultimate goal of using LinkedIn is to develop strong relationships that help you to advance your professional objectives.

The first step to developing powerful relationships on LinkedIn is to *fully complete your profile page*. This will give your profile a better chance of standing out to potential connections. The key to any good relationship is that it be mutually beneficial. It should be clear to potential contacts when they look at your profile why they should want to build a professional relationship with you.

The Most Important Sections of your Profile to complete are the:

- **Summary**
- **Experience**
- **Education**
- **Honors and Awards**

Also, it is important that you *emphasize results and skills*, rather than dates and titles.

To start with you will want to add contacts that you know well and who know you such as:

• **Former Employers**
• **Co-workers**
• **Professors**
• **Classmates**

Each time that you add a new contact, you should write them a recommendation and then ask for one in return. Having *recommendations* will make your profile stand out to potential new connections more than anything else.

After you have acquired some contacts and recommendations, you should then join *LinkedIn Groups.* Make sure that you join groups in the specific areas of interest that you want to build your network. Now that you've joined the right groups, you share a common interest with some of the top people in your field. This will make it more likely that they will accept your unsolicited connection requests.

The best way to make a good connection is to be become a resource to them. Promote your contacts businesses. Put links to their sites on your websites and blogs. Write recommendations for them. Comments on their posts and answer their questions and polls.

Becoming a valuable resource to your LinkedIn connections creates a reason for them to expand your relationship or to interact with you "offline". Escalating your relationship with influential connections beyond LinkedIn can be the key to landing your "dream client", promoting your business or landing a lucrative new project. In summary, you build strong relationships on LinkedIn by creating a powerful *Profile*, strategically joining the right *Groups*, acquiring the right *Connections* and *Recommendations* and becoming a resource rather than just a contact. If you follow these steps, you can build powerful LinkedIn relationships that can dramatically enhance your professional success.

How to Design an Effective Business Brochure to Promote Your Brand

by **Vince Rogers**

It can be difficult to explain to potential customers specifically what value you can bring to their business. Your "elevator pitch", your business card or even a well crafted letter may not be sufficient. A well designed Marketing Brochure for your business can be the most effective tool that you have in your Marketing arsenal. If done effectively, a good brochure can help you to make an impression on a potential client and stand out from the competition.

An effective brochure for your business must combine 4 vital elements to successfully communicate your marketing message:

• Attractive Images
• Clear Layout
• Simple Folding
• Strong Writing

Attractive Images will be the first thing that catches a prospects eye. Strong images are what initially hold the reader's attention. While images should be eye-catching, they must also be appropriate to the business that you are promoting.

The layout of your brochure must be clear and have a logical flow. This will enable it to be read easily and completely. The reader must also be able to unfold and re-fold the brochure in a way that makes it easy to use over and over again.

The goal of a good brochure is to communicate a lot of important information without using a lot of words. Therefore, the writing must be strong, clear, logical and concise. Also, make sure that your vital contact information is prominently displayed and easy to read. Don't forget to include your:

• Mailing address.

• Phone numbers

• Fax number.

• E-Mail address.

• Web Site address.

• Social Media Information

Although you want your brochure to stand out and be noticed, you should avoid using any fonts, graphics or colors that make the actual content difficult to read. You may decide to design the brochure yourself or you may use another company to produce it. In any event, you should pay careful attention to making sure that you incorporate all of these elements into making the most effective marketing brochure possible.

Connecting Mission to Brand:
The Evolution of a Modern Non-Profit
by Vince Rogers

In 1920, the *National Urban League* assumed its current formal name. This national organization was created through the consolidation of several prominent empowerment organizations of that era. They adopted as their mission, *"to enable African Americans to secure economic self-reliance, parity, power and civil rights."* The Atlanta chapter – the *Atlanta Urban League* was also formed that same year.

Most people usually associate an effective branding strategy with *creating identity (brand awareness)* and *establishing image*. In the case of a non-profit organization, effective branding must accomplish much more than that. The branding strategy must also be carefully aligned with the mission and values of the organization. A successful branding strategy must also facilitate the expansion of the organization's *operating capacity (capacity building)* and be representative of the organization's *social impact*.

Successful modern non-profits must evolve. When they do, they must also make sure that their branding strategy be connected to their renewed mission. The mission of the Urban League has always been economic empowerment and civil rights. The primary measurement of the organization's social impact was finding job opportunities for their constituency. The Urban League realized that simply securing job opportunities in this evolving economy did not effectively address their mission. The "League" has responded to changing times and identified that the true measurement of success should now be establishing businesses and creating jobs. At the vanguard of realizing this renewed mission is the *Atlanta Entrepreneurship Center* **www.aultec.org**

Providing dynamic leadership at the helm of the Atlanta Entrepreneurship Center is their *Executive Director – Mr. Marc Parham.* As he so eloquently and succinctly states, *"Finding people jobs has always been the mission of the Urban League"*, but this was essentially a process of negotiating for or demanding jobs from mainstream employers. This was necessary to redress inequities that developed because of past civil rights and social welfare injustices. However, according to Parham the charge of the organization as a modern non-profit is to now *"Create jobs via entrepreneurship"*.

The Atlanta Entrepreneurship Center is one very important component of a holistic approach to providing economic empowerment programs to the National Urban Leagues' constituency. The Entrepreneurship Center (TEC) was launched in Atlanta in October 2004. At the core of the program is education via four primary methods. These essential training programs are as follows;

- Start-up Business Essentials Series for Entrepreneurs
- Existing Business Series – Writing The Business Plan
- Specialized Workshops - Focusing on specific topics (i.e. QuickBooks, Websites, Insurance, Access to Capital, etc)
- Group or One on One Coaching – Experienced Business Consultants will meet one on one with participants to coach them with the development of their business plan.

The different components are designed to suit the needs of start-up, early stage and long-established business. The *Start-up Business Essentials Series* is a six (6) session series that helps entrepreneurs to understand the basic business essentials for starting a business. The *Existing Business Series* curriculum is devoted to giving entrepreneurs a foundation in the *"Core 4 Systems"* which are:

- Success Planning
- Marketing Planning
- Cash-flow Planning
- Operations Planning

While for-profit *"business incubators"* may offer similar services, a non-profit is uniquely positioned to provide participants with additional value added components. They can offer a high caliber of business acumen, lower cost and provide other "supportive services'. Many top-notch Atlanta business consultants make themselves available to students as their way of "giving back". According to Parham, *"People who work at the Urban League, really understand, the plight of the people that they work with because they've walked in their shoes."* Essentially this means that they have also experienced all of the ups and downs of building a successful business. They are motivated to share their wealth of knowledge in order to help other people succeed, not by the prospect of personal gain.

In developing a branding strategy for a non-profit, it may be necessary to first undertake an *Analysis of* the organization. SWOT stands for *Strengths, Weaknesses,*

43

Opportunities and Threats. This is important in order to access whether reengineering the branding strategy could possibly undermine the already established *brand equity* of the organization. Brand equity is the value that a company realizes in the public from positive associations by consumers compared to their competition. In the case of a non-profit organization, alienating long time supporters could possibly alienate existing supporters and damage the ability to realize ongoing *social impact.* Providing social impact is ultimately the purpose of an effective non-profit.

In the case of a non-profit, not all of the impacts are always tangibly measureable. Mr. Parham asserts that a significant aspect of aligning the branding strategy of the Atlanta Entrepreneurship Center to their mission is to *"Give people the confidence that they can succeed."* Unlike a business, accomplishing an intangible goal such as this enhances brand equity and is an important sign that a non-profit organization is succeeding. Enhancing brand equity while demonstrating social impact is ultimately the goal of connecting mission to brand.

A Personal Branding Strategy for Your Career Search
by **Vince Rogers**

In this turbulent economy, companies still face the challenge of maximizing productivity. Essential to achieving that mission is making cost effective, purchase decisions that add value to the "bottom line". Effective managers must maximize return on investment from every resource – especially human resources. Therefore, making excellent hiring decisions is critical to achieving the success of an organization.

The goal of employers in today's job market is to find the "ideal" candidate for every job opening. Facing a "lean" job market, the goal of every jobseeker should be to present themselves as the ideal candidate for a specific career opportunity. From the employer's perspective, finding the right person for a job is not just a hiring decision – it is also a purchase decision. Therefore, it is imperative that you package yourself in a way that makes you more attractive than all of the other "products" available in the marketplace.

Employers want to know more than whether you can simply do the job. It is also necessary that you can align with the mission, values and philosophy of the company. Are you an *Experienced I.T. Professional* or a *Technology Industry Change Agent*? Different organizations may require or desire one or the other. However if you're not the right fit for the specific opportunity you're applying for, the savvy hiring manager will know. Most importantly, you don't want to waste your time applying for one position, if you are really better suited to another one that is available elsewhere. Many unfocused jobseekers apply over and over again for positions that they're not suited for, expecting to sneak in the back door. Well here's an important newsflash – savvy employers aren't "buying it".

It is essential that you identify and effectively communicate your *Brand Promise*. This is your statement or statements that combine what you are, with what you can deliver to the company. Anybody can say *"I am a hard working professional who has produced quality results"* and many people make such generic statements all of the time. My advice is that you go in another direction. I would suggest something more like: *"I am a Technology Industry Change Agent who works well with teams and independently, to solve complex problems and maximize the productivity of a dynamic I.T. Department."* This type of Brand Promise distinguishes your uniqueness and establishes the value you will bring to the organization.

In addition to creating a customized resume and cover letter for each position, you should also be prepared to make a full presentation of your entire Career Portfolio. Written letters of recommendation; copies of awards and certificates as well as documentation of academic achievements should be made available upon the request of the prospective employer. All of these items can be compiled into a "Brag Book" A "Brag Book" is a binder or folder containing documentation of your academic and career accomplishments that you can present to a job interviewer. It effectively serves the same presentation function as a business's portfolio, which one company would provide to another in a Business to Business or "B2B" setting.

In the final analysis, an individual must undertake many of the same steps to get their next job as a business does in order to get their next client. So just like a businessperson, you should also create a business card and start actively networking. Although "Job Boards", social and professional networking sites and even blogging are great outlets for showcasing your personal brand, most new career opportunities are discovered through "face-to-face" Networking. Nevertheless, whether it is online or in person, utilizing the aforementioned strategies will set you apart from the competition in the execution of an effective personal branding strategy for career success.

Place Branding - The Case for "Yo Boulevard!"
by Vince Rogers

Place Branding is a fairly new concept in the branding *"discipline"*. The term refers to the process of communicating a well-crafted image to a target audience in order to create a specific perception of a particular place. Most often place branding is the aide-decamp of Branding's close relative – Reputation Management. Reputation Management is the process of formulating a positive image or repairing a negative image of a brand. Most often a brand accrues a bad reputation following a negative event or unfortunate change in circumstances.

In the case of a place, whether it is a nation, a city or a neighborhood, this bad reputation usually evolves over time. It ultimately can lead to losses of population, declining economic activity and high crime rates. A negative perception can be associated with a place for years, even if the facts don't support the perception. This in summary is what has become the plight of Atlanta's Old Fourth Ward.

The neighborhood is home to Martin Luther King Jr.'s childhood home, Ebenezer Baptist Church and in years past, was considered a very desirable residential location in Atlanta. Today the principal through street in this community - Boulevard, has earned a reputation for facilitating every urban vice imaginable. According to Kwanza Hall the presiding Atlanta City Councilmember for the district, it is *"the most concentrated pocket of poverty in the southeastern United States."*

There are several cities in America such as Detroit on the negative end of the spectrum and Miami on the positive end of the spectrum that have experienced a change in perception over the years. So what can be done to change the perception of a place when the fortunes of the community have reversed? There are essentially 4 Key Steps to a implementing a successful Place Branding Strategy:

1. **Assemble a Diverse Team of Advisers**
2. **Partner with the Business Community in the surrounding area**
3. **Concentrate on Achieving Key Objectives**
4. **Leverage Existing Community Assets**

TEDx Atlanta - The Birth of the Yo Boulevard! Brand

In March of 2012, Councilman Hall was as an attendee at a TEDx Atlanta **www.tedxatlanta.com**conference. Surrounded by some of the best and brightest minds in the city, it dawned on him that he should seize the opportunity to seek confederates for his campaign to restore civility to Boulevard. In January, Hall had already declared 2012 the *"Year of Boulevard"*. It was at the conference that the brand name *"Yo Boulevard!"* **www.yoboulevard.com** evolved and became a living breathing entity. The association with TEDx Atlanta served the purpose of gaining access to a diverse source of advisers with vast intellectual capital. It also provided the potential for partnerships with the city's most progressive business leaders who possessed the necessary physical and financial capital.

The Children Are Our Future

Hall determined that the most important objective that should be pursued was empowering the children who lived in the community to break the *"cycle of poverty"*. He decided to focus on the children as the key objective because he believes that *"You can change all the physical structures, but if you haven't given people real opportunities, all you're going to do is push them out."* Borne out of the TEDx conference, a three (3) part challenge was issued to the business and community leaders in the community:

1. **Sponsor a child for summer camp**
2. **Hire a child for a summer internship**
3. **Help a young person start a business and become an entrepreneur**

During what was termed as the *"Summer of Possibility"* in association with their diverse team of advisers and by leveraging local businesses and vital community assets, Yo Boulevard! achieved all three objectives.

Operation PEACE: A Diamond in a Rough Place

Facing the onslaught of "gentrification" and the specter of past "urban renewal" schemes, it is unlikely that the residents in the Boulevard corridor would have welcomed warmly a new round of infiltration by people they consider "outsiders". Even the inroads of more affluent or well educated residents of the adjacent communities might be met with skepticism without the intercession of an established and trusted force in the community. The natural candidate to fill this role in the Boulevard community was Operation P.E.A.C.E.**www.operationpeace.org**

Under the steadfast and trusted leadership of Executive Director, Ms. Edna Moffett, since 1995 Operation P.E.A.C.E. has been a dynamic agent of change in an otherwise neglected community. Operation P.E.A.C.E began as an effort to improve the lives of the children in the Old Fourth Ward community. In addition to serving as a buffer between the neighborhood children and the negative forces at work in the community, the organization has evolved into the primary community resource for residents looking for solutions to their problems. According to Moffet, *"Because of our long track record as a catalyst for change in the community and a driver of successful outcomes for our youth, it was decided that Operation P.E.A.C.E. should be the standard-bearer for Yo Boulevard!"*

"Living Laboratory for Innovation"

Only time, effort and "right action" will determine whether Yo Boulevard! can effectively counteract years of negative perceptions of the Old Fourth Ward community and the infamous Boulevard corridor. Hall's stated goal is to convert the community into a *"Living Laboratory for Innovation". Hi*s prudent insight and stalwart commitment to the project are evidenced by his observations that *"We're talking about changing something that's been in place for thirty years. It's not going to change in six months."* Although place branding initiatives have an inherent idealistic quality, with the type of pragmatic leadership that Councilman Hall provides to the project, it stands an excellent chance of succeeding.

Any successful branding strategy requires the dedication of adequate time, resources and organization. In the case of Place Branding, it is best to move moderately rather than be overly aggressive. The alliances that have been forged can be broken and confidences of the various stakeholders can be easily eroded. Yet if managed properly, an area that was thought to have already seen its best days can be transformed into a vigorous, lively and productive community.

Reputation Management – Imagining a "New Morehouse"
by **Vince Rogers**

Reputation Management is the process of repairing the public perception of a brand that has experienced some kind of reputation changing occurrence. Companies and persons who do not respond quickly to such incidents can suffer irreparable damage. Venerable old companies such as American Airlines, British Petroleum and Ford Motors have suffered reputation damaging scandals that have led to bankruptcy, the loss of millions of dollars and the discontinuation of popular product models. Currently, the U.S. Presidential election may be decided based on one candidate's ability to reverse the negative perceptions caused by remarks that he made in a "leaked" video.

In some cases, a decline in the reputation of an organization can have consequences for the institution as well as other associated *"stakeholders"*. Scandals within such respected institutions as the Catholic Church, the Boy Scouts of America and Penn State University have produced consequences for the reputation and brand perception of the current members, past participants and even affect the perceived value of the degrees earned by the alumni of the respective school. In the case of one's *Alma Mater*, the associated *Brand Equity* that is derived from the association of being an alumnus of certain institutions has a direct affect on your personal brand. When it comes to such positive associations, being know as a *"Morehouse Man"* is one of the strongest personal branding attributes one can possess next to being an *"Ivy Leaguer"*.

Since the founding of Morehouse College in 1867, it has been regarded as the standard of excellence with respect to educating Black men in America. Alumni of the college include Nobel Laureate Martin Luther King, Jr., former Republican Presidential Candidate Herman Cain and former U.S. Surgeon General David Satcher. While other predominantly Black colleges are facing the threat of closure and an ongoing conversation focused on their continued relevance, the Morehouse brand is still very highly regarded. Yet Morehouse is not immune from the economic and cultural threats facing other Historically Black Colleges and Universities (or *HBCU*s) as well as institutions of higher learning in general.

In 2009, Morehouse College introduced a dress code to be adhered to by current students in order to reinvigorate the image of a well dressed, well groomed, well mannered Morehouse student. These attributes had always been associated with the *"Morehouse Mystique"*. Although many people (alumni in particular) regarded this move as a positive one, many current students saw this as a threat to the expression of their individuality. Individual expression is also something that was a long held precept of the *Renaissance man* building tradition of the school. The administration took an alternative position, asserting that a *"Morehouse Man"* should want to differentiate himself from the prevailing *"hip-hop* "inspired fashion trends favored by other young men. To the contrary, many students asserted that given the hefty price tag that they pay for tuition, their sartorial expression should certainly be their own choice. Yet the dress code issue revealed an even more onerous issue that had long been bubbling below the surface and influenced the internal and external perception of Morehouse, current students and alumni.

In the October 2010 issue of *Vibe Magazine* an article appeared entitled *"The Mean Girls of Morehouse"*. In this article openly homosexual students asserted that the dress code issue was raised as a tacit ploy to restrict the civil liberties of gay students. Because Morehouse College is an all-male institution, the issue of homosexuality is one that has always impacted the school's reputation and brand. Negative associations with homosexuality have changed over time with evolving cultural attitudes towards homosexuality, yet negative perceptions regarding homosexuality may never disappear completely. However, more disturbing than the idea that a group of students might be targeted for discrimination by the college, is the notion that any group of students may be the targets of civil rights inequities at the school regarded by some as the birthplace of the American *"Civil Rights Movement"*.

Alumni of Morehouse College were instrumental in the founding of the *Southern Christian Leadership Conference (SCLC)*, the *Student Non-Violent Coordinating Committee (SNCC)* as well as the election of the first Black mayor of the city of Atlanta, Maynard Jackson. A sense of obligation to fellow man, a sense of mission to improve society and a tradition of working for social justice have always been regarded as part of the Morehouse tradition. Since the issues of the dress code, gay rights, a less publicized Moody's Investors Service debt downgrade and other issues have been raised, Morehouse has been *"under the microscope"*. The college finds itself in a position where another blow to the reputation of the school might prove fatal.

Earlier this year, a group of current and former students recognized the precarious situation of their beloved school and decided to make an organized response. They responded by penning a *"Collective Statement"* that was presented to the Board of Trustees of Morehouse College. This effort was spearheaded by alumnus Imar Hutchins. Hutchins states that he was motivated to take these actions because, *"The current state of Morehouse is unsustainable and if present trends continue – societally, financially, educationally and organizationally – the College will fail to be viable one day."* The *"Collective Statement"* raises six **(6)** issues that they urged the board to address in terms of assuring the long-term viability of the institution: They are as follows:

1) A continued commitment to the core values of the organization

2) Defending the "value proposition" of the "brand"

3) The effective allocation of the current and future resources of the organization

4) Financial transparency of the organization

5) Assuring the quality of the product (academic rigor)

6) Demonstrating a commitment to diversity

All of these concerns represent the types of issues that internal and external stakeholders should always be concerned with in regard to maintaining the reputation and brand equity of any organization that they support. Hopefully over time and with hard work and cooperation between current students, alumni, supporters and the administration, all interested stakeholders can work together to do even more than just imagine a *"New Morehouse"*. Hopefully, they will soon be successful in bringing into being a stronger, more viable and eternally relevant Morehouse College that will endure

for centuries to come.

Alert the Media! – Using On-line Press Releases to Promote Your Personal Brand

by **Vince Rogers**

What if you did something that was really important. Something that people actually needed to know about. How would you get the word out?

These days, social media sites are flooded with self promoters posting links, "tweeting tweets" and sharing stories about their various accomplishments. Many of these stories may be entertaining, but they aren't really newsworthy. On top of that, the news cycle for social media can only be a few minutes and reach only a relatively small amount of people. Most of the people who do see it are usually people who you already know. They would probably find out about your great news anyway. So how do you get your message across to a broad audience of people who can truly benefit from the information?

Sometimes to really get your message out there, you may have to resort to using tried and true media sources. However, unless you are already a well known celebrity or prominent organization, finding newspapers, magazines, and radio or television stations that will cover your great "news" may be an uphill battle. On the other hand, with the emerging popularity of "new media", bloggers and the aforementioned social media options, traditional media outlets are also under some pressure to find fresh news ideas. As a tactic for building your personal brand, a powerful way to gain media attention for you story is to issue an online press release.

Online press release services such as PRLog; PRweb and i-Newswire offer various free and paid distribution packages. These platforms make it easy for Public Relations non-professionals to create professional looking press releases. If you think your news is of a higher level and you have expectations that it will raise your profile significantly, you may want to hire a professional to create and distribute your press release. However, with either route you take, there is no guarantee that your press release will be picked up by the media.

The most essential factor in determining if your press release is picked up by the media is whether it truly lives up to the most narrowly defined definition of "news". Sometimes determining what is news and what is not can be a very "grey area". For instance, announcing a sale at your store is not news. However, announcing that you will give away a new car to a selected shopper during a sale at your store is news. Examples of other possible newsworthy events are as follows:

- Introducing New Product or Service Offerings
- Top Management Promotion or Retirement Announcements
- Getting Published in a Prestigious Publication
- New Plant or Retail Outlet Openings or Closings
- Sponsorship or Hosting of Charity Events or Fundraisers

Now here's the bad news. Even when the information is truly newsworthy your press release still may not get picked up. Now here's the good news. Issuing press releases can help you build your brand in other ways. The circulation of the press release can enhance your *SEO (Search Engine Optimization)* which is a measure of the effectiveness and reach of your online presence. Also, your press release may be read by other audiences such as organizations looking for an expert speaker, or a potential new client or employer. Press releases may be a tool from the "Stone Age", but they are still a powerful tool that can be used to build your personal brand today.

Adult Education:

Using Online Learning to Raise Your Human Capital

by **Vince Rogers**

You couldn't go to college after high school. So you started working. Then you started a family, had kids, and even bought a home. You've done okay for yourself, but you believe you could do even better. You try to move up higher in your company, but all of the good jobs require a college degree. You finally come to the conclusion that you have no other choice but to go back to school. Egads! – School at this age?

You envision walking into a crowded classroom and sitting in an uncomfortable desk for hours after a hard day's work. Even worse is the idea of studying on your weekends off. You struggle to stay awake and try to learn something from this guy standing in the front of the room. Your "professor" is a half interested part-time teacher who took this job for the same reasons you're going back to school. Now you feel even more out of place when you look around this room full of slackers whose parents are paying their way to attend yet another almost Alma Mater. They're just hoping that they may someday move out of the basement – the parents that is. The kid could care less.

Fortunately, this is a scene from the olden days. No not the Middle Ages when only the elite were able to go to college. It is a memory from a mere 30 years ago when only a few totally online college courses were first offered. New York Institute of Technology purportedly offered the first "virtual campus" through their *American Open University of*

NYIT in 1984. In 1996 Jones International University lays claim to launching the first regionally accredited fully online university in the United States.

Eventually, online-education would become a serious alternative for many prospective students. This was in large part due to the successful branding strategy of the University of Phoenix. Founded in 1976 as a traditional college for what was then referred to as *"non-traditional"* students *"Phoenix"* would ultimately set the standard for on-line education.

The non-traditional student moniker was used to refer to those students who didn't for various reasons make a direct path to college after high school. Nowadays, according to a 2002 National Center for Education Statistics (NCES) report, *"nontraditional students make up 73 percent of all students enrolled in undergraduate programs, and 39 percent of all undergraduate students are 25 years or older."*Delaying college attendance was once thought to be the exception, now it has now become commonplace.

The University of Phoenix was founded by the pioneer of "for profit" education, John Sperling. He believed that *"working adult students were often invisible on traditional campuses and treated as second-class citizens."* The University of Phoenix started their online program in 1989. The program became very attractive by providing students from all over the country with the ability to gain a college degree from a "name-brand" recognized academic institution. However, over time the success of "Phoenix" opened the door to institutions that weren't as reputable as their authentic sounding names might suggest. They offered academic instruction and engaged in financial practices that were not nearly of the same high-caliber.

For many years most traditional colleges and universities saw the online path as a distinctly separate way to earn a college degree. Eventually, many would have a change of philosophy and become responsive to offering the on-line model. They recognized that the internet did not just represent competition for classroom instruction, but opportunity for traditional colleges. It would ultimately be seen as yet another way that students could gain an education in a changing world. Now through such programs as the Harvard Extension School and the CIT (Computer Information Technology) program at the University of Southern California, students young and old, working or unemployed or working toward a first Bachelor's or PhD. can earn a degree online from the most legitimate providers.

One of the most innovative programs for on-line education exists through the consortium of public colleges and universities located in Georgia. *GeorgiaONmyLINE* **www.georgiaonmyline.org** provides access to *"....public higher education, [by] providing you with a database of online and distance education programs offered through the 31 accredited institutions within the University System of Georgia."* It is a truly innovative idea that enables the possibility for a young person to gain the credentials to enter the growing healthcare industry by earning an Associates of Science in Nursing at Georgia Perimeter College. On the other end of the spectrum, a busy City Planner could potentially earn a Doctor of Public Administration degree from the prestigious Valdosta State University – the flagship sports powerhouse of *TitleTown USA* which ESPN named Valdosta, Georgia in 2008.

GeorgiaOnmyLine represents some of the most innovative thinking in "higher learning" today. With GeorgiaOnmyLine, there exist no concerns about the quality or accreditation of the school, or the price and affordability of the programs. In most cases the courses are taught by regular instructors and the costs are the same as the on-campus options. Also, rather than individually researching the hundreds of programs offered at the various University System of Georgia schools, GeorgiaOnmyLine serves as a central sources for access to information about all of the on-line programs offered at the various state schools. Students can also use the website to:

- Research Georgia's 31 public institutions offering online higher education programs
- Browse through degree programs and courses, including details such as admissions processes, tuition, technical requirements and credit hours
- Search for programs at the associate's, bachelor's, master's, and certificate levels that fit your specific educational and lifestyle-related needs
- Streamline and simplify the process of finding the right program for you

GeorgiaOnmyLine also provides students who may not be sure if college is right for them with an opportunity to try the coursework out in the comfort of their own home. Older students, working adults, persons with disabilities and others with physical challenges may find the on-line environment more conducive to learning and earning a college degree. While pursuing your Bachelors of Science degree in Education at the University of Georgia, unfortunately you may miss out on watching the "Dawgs" flounce the Florida Gators "between the hedges". On the other hand, you won't have to worry about finding your roommates pet iguana in your sock drawer while you earn your Masters in Computer Science degree at Georgia Tech. All things considered, GeorgiaOnmyLine provides students from across Georgia with the opportunity to attend some of the most prestigious universities in the world, while earning some of the most useful college degrees available today.

For more information please visit **www.georgiaonmyline.org**

20 Questions – Identifying Your Brand Personality
by **Vince Rogers**

Many of us have played the game *20 Questions*. In this game of deductive reasoning, multiple questioners ask up to 20 questions to a single person. The person must ultimately reveal the secret answer that they are holding onto, if the questioners ask the right questions. Asking the right questions can help you to reveal the secrets to discovering your *Brand Personality* as well.

In their efforts to empower clients, Alphonso Whitfield and Margaret Diggs of Waycross, Georgia based **The Vital Portal www.thevitalportal.com** have devised 20 essential questions that you can also use to help uncover your Brand Personality. According to Whitfield, the Vital Portal is used by *"ventures of all sizes to climb the business conditions learning curve quickly and efficiently."* Investopedia defines Brand Personality as *"A set of human characteristics that are attributed to a brand name."* Therefore, when it comes to building a Personal Brand, understanding your Brand Personality means understanding YOU.

The 20 Questions that the team at Vital has devised are as follows:

1) What did you aspire to be as a child?

2) If you could meet anyone in the world, living or dead, who would it be?

3) What would you say to them?

4) What is your vision of a perfect team?

5) Give us your definition of success.

6) Tell us about the best part of your work.

7) What keeps you awake at night?

8) If you could be a dessert, what would you be and why?

9) What is your favorite word or phrase, the one you tend to use most often?

10) Walk us through a typical day at your current/previous position.

11) Who has been most influential in your life?

12) If you could go back to a specific era in history, which one would you choose and why?

13) What have been the biggest disappointments of your career?

14) What is your favorite way to relax after a long hard day at work?

15) Tell us how you think five co-workers/team members would describe you.

16) What career accomplishments are you most proud of?

17) What are/were your favorite things about your current/previous position?

18) What made you choose this occupation?

19) What behavior(s) did you inherit from your parents?

20) What would be the FIRST thing you would do if you knew today was your last day?

The answers to these 20 Questions can help you to gather the vital information that you need to understand your Brand Personality. Understanding your Brand Personality is an essential, yet often overlooked component of building your Personal Brand. These 20 Questions were designed by Vital to help you gather the information you will need to navigate this process successfully.

Information is without a doubt the most important of my *Six Keys to Success*. Obtaining the right data in order to make the best possible decisions (not the most conveniently available data) is the key to formulating a winning *Success Strategy*. This is true whether you are embarking on a personal endeavor, a professional enterprise or taking a risk in any area of your life in which you are seeking to be successful. Ultimately, if you input good data into the formulation of your *Success Plan*, chances are excellent that you will end up with a plan that should lead you to your desired result.

Using "LinkedIn Skills" to Showcase Your "Personal Product & Service Offerings"

by **Vince Rogers**

In February of 2011, LinkedIn **www.linkedin.com**introduced **LinkedIn**

Skills www.linkedin.com/skills LinkedIn Skills is a special section that enables users

to showcase their *"Skills & Expertise".* In today's economy, the ability to communicate

your skills and talents is more important than just merely listing your career positions

and job duties - no matter how impressive they might be. As stated by **Pete**

Skomoroch an official LinkedIn blogger, *"....To succeed in the talent economy, it is*

crucial to showcase your skills and....the expertise you need to get the job done."

Just like any other enterprise, building your Personal Brand consists of identifying your

product and service offerings. Your *"Personal Product & Service Offerings"* may be

as simple as Meat Processing or as complex as Investment Banking. Whatever your

skills and abilities may be, it is important that they accurately reflect what you have to

offer. The salable skills and areas of expertise that you claim to have, they represent the

personal goods and services that you have in inventory for sale to a potential consumer.

Also, it is important that they be relevant to the type of opportunity that you are

pursuing.

To access the Skills and Expertise section and add it you your profile, you must follow

these steps:

69

1) Log in to your **LinkedIn Profile**

2) Locate the **Recommended for you** section on the right side of the screen and Add **(+)** the **Skills & Expertise** section to your profile

3) Select **Edit Profile**

4) Scroll down to the Skills & Expertise section

5) Click **"Edit"** to **Add & Remove Skills** and **Manage Endorsements**

As far as Endorsements are concerned, their usefulness is debatable. They may or may not have an impact on people who view your profile. In many cases, persons who endorse your skills may be familiar with you, but unfamiliar with your career aptitudes. However, the exercise of building your list of Skills & Expertise is primarily meant to help you to take a personal inventory. Gaining and utilizing endorsements is a secondary strategy.

In the upcoming series of articles that comprise the ***"Creating Your Personal Brand: A 12 Step Success Plan"*** series, we will discuss a comprehensive strategy for *Evaluating Your Skills and Talents*. In the meantime, making effective use of the "LinkedIn Skills" section is a powerful way to understand and promote your "Personal Product & Service Offerings". Building your list of "Skills & Expertise" will help you to understand what you have to offer to the world. It will also help viewers to synthesize the other content in your powerful LinkedIn profile.

Using Toastmasters International to Become a
Competent Personal Brand Communicator
by Vince Rogers

It has been said that _Public Speaking_ is the greatest fear of most people. This is very unfortunate, because public speaking is probably the ultimate tool that can be used to establish your _Personal Brand_. Actually, getting to the point where you are sought after to speak publicly signals that you have accomplished the ultimate goal of Personal Branding – achieving _"Brand Leadership"_. According to **www.businessdictionary.com** Brand Leadership is defined as becoming the _"....Most widely....recognized product in a particular market segment...."_ The kids these days would call that being a _"Boss"_.

So what do you do if you are ready to take that step into the Public Speaking "arena", but you have yet to conquer the fear? Well one strategy is to just find an audience and start speaking. Even if you could find the courage to do that, how do you find a willing audience if you have yet to become a sought after spokesperson? Since 1924 many aspiring orators have joined _Toastmasters_ **International** as a resource to use for _"....developing public speaking and leadership skills through practice and feedback in local clubs...."_

Toastmasters succeeds in empowering speakers by providing them with constructive audience feedback in an environment of mutual encouragement. According to their website **www.toastmasters.org** *"A Toastmasters meeting is a learn-by-doing workshop in which participants hone their speaking and leadership skills in a no-pressure atmosphere."* Over time, members progress towards the goal of becoming a *"Competent Communicator"* by:

1) Utilizing the constructive Feedback provided through peer Evaluations.

2) Confronting their fears by regularly making impromptu presentations.

3) Managing the various aspects of making effective presentations by Conducting Meetings.

4) Progressing through the self-paced *"Competent Communication Manual"*.

The **Competent Communication Manual** is the essential foundation of the Toastmasters program.

I recently visited a local Toastmasters Club in order to witness the process firsthand. I was invited to the *Cascade United Toastmasters Club* by their newly elected *Vice President of Membership, Ms. Alison Gibson.* It was clear to me that the Toastmasters method was effective in helping members to manage their fear of public speaking and build their communication skills. The reasons why each individual joins Toastmasters are different. In Alison's case, she proclaims that she wanted to among other things *"....improve my listening skills...."*

Joining a Toastmaster Club is a very straightforward process. There are essentially 3 Steps:

Step 1; Find/Visit a Club **www.toastmasters.org/findaclub**

Step 2; Ask the Vice President of Membership for an application.

Step 3; Return the completed application and dues to the VP of Membership.

There is a customary $20 **New Members Fee**, plus a $36 bi-annual **International Dues** payment. There may also be club dues, which vary from club to club.

Personally, I found the experience to be as advertised. I was even drafted into service to give feedback about different aspects of the meeting. For most people, the combination of immersion, participation, support and encouragement has proven to be an effective method for alleviating the fear of public speaking and acquiring the necessary skills to become a competent public communicator. Consistently engaging in this process should ultimately lead to gaining the tools needed to become an in-demand public presenter and cementing your *Personal Brand Leadership*.

To learn more please visit **www.toastmasters.org**

Taking Your Personal Brand "Global"
Through Networking and Publishing
by Vince Rogers

The *Bard of Avon* once famously alleged that *"Some are born great, some achieve greatness, and some have greatness thrust upon them."* Few would argue with William Shakespeare being considered as an authority on greatness. When it comes to being an authority on writing and books, Bill usually gets the last word as well. Yet a prolific writer residing in the modern *"A-Town"* has attempted to best the Bard – at least on the subject of Greatness.

Atlanta based motivational author and entertainment impresario Germaine Moody - the self proclaimed *"King of Networking"*, has produced the most ambitious book ever on the subject of Greatness. In the book *"50 Seeds of Greatness"www.50seedsofgreatness.com* Moody addresses 50 vital topics that can empower readers to *"....produce an abundance of whatever we desire, while also leaving a legacy of our presence on Earth."* However what makes the book so remarkable is that he also amassed almost *400 Contributors* from over *100 Countries* around the world to take part in the project. This extraordinary accomplishment is currently being considered for inclusion in the **Guinness Book of World Records** as the largest and most international publishing undertaking of all-time.

By writing this book, Mr. Moody has also come up with an ingenious way to expand his brand. This high-profile endeavor has enabled him to network with other movers and shakers around the world. The way that he accomplished this was by issuing an International call for authors to contribute their own thoughts about greatness to the book. Contributors from around the world were asked to answer the question *"What does Greatness mean to me?"* He presented this invitation primarily via *LinkedIn*. This enabled him to exponentially expand his network of professional contacts, while also creating an International marketing campaign for the book and acquiring high quality content for the project.

I was among the change agents and thought leaders who were asked to contribute their definition of greatness to the project. In addition to contributors from Atlanta and the United States, the book includes words of wisdom from as far away as Albania and Zambia. By showcasing a wide ranging group of contributors, it is insured that readers will be exposed to an unusually broad array of insight and wisdom.

Undertaking this project is clear evidence that Germaine Moody may very well be the King of Networking. He is a dedicated *"networker"* who believes that *"....Networking is essential, no matter who you are, where you are and no matter what industry you work in...."* Aspiring pretenders to his throne can definitely learn a lesson or 50 from the *"King"* On the subject of networking, Moody goes on to say that *"People will always be your greatest assets and resources, in business and in life."*

In keeping with his dedication to the business of networking, he has already moved on to his next equally ambitious publishing and networking project. His upcoming book *"The Networking Bible"* (due April 2014) reveals fundamental keys and secrets to networking. One of the most important strategies that he will cover in the new book is *"Gaining access to your greatest influencers"*. In addition to his publishing projects, Moody also operates a vast networking group dedicated to the **Atlanta Entertainment Industry**@ LinkedIn.com. It is clear that if you are a student of greatness, a practitioner of networking or you aspire to number yourself among the Atlanta entertainment industry elite, Germaine Moody – "The King of Networking" is a person you need to know.

To learn more about the ***50 Seeds of Greatness*** book please visit ***www.50seedsofgreatness.com*** and to network with ***Germaine Moody, "The King of Networking"*** visit ***www.linkedin.com/in/germainemoody***

Using Pinterest to Promote Your Personal Brand Identity

by **Vince Rogers**

To some people, Pinterest **www.pinterest.com** is the most esoteric of the four major Social Networking sites. Maybe esoteric is not the right word. What would be a better way to put it? Okay, some people just don't get Pinterest at all.

On the other hand, according to **www.ebizmba.com**an estimated 85 million users absolutely love Pinterest. They have earned this position by surpassing upstart Google Plus and the pioneering MySpace. They have achieved this impressive milestone in just a little over 3 years of being in business. While avid users may love it, some may still wonder what is the point to all of this "Pinning". Well rather than offer my personal opine on this point, let's hear from the people at Pinterest about what it means to be a pinner.

Pinning, Re-Pinning and Liking

A *"Pin"* is simply an interesting image or video. According to the Pinterest powers that be, *"Pinterest is a tool for collecting and organizing things you love."* These beloved pics and clips are collected, organized and shared onto *"Boards"*.

There are 3 ways to add a Pin to a Board:

1) You may upload a Pin from your computer

2) You may add a Pin from a website by copying and pasting a link

3) You may install the *"Pin It"* button to your browser to Pin directly from a website

Pinners access the Pinterest main page and scroll through pins that have been pinned by their "Friends" and onto boards that they follow. Pins are displayed chronologically as they are pinned. You may also perform keyword specific searches for pins. The way that you share pins of other users is by either *"Re-pinning"* them onto your boards or *"Liking"* them onto your page. There are two ways to expand the number of people that you share your pins with:

1) Finding your friends from other social networks who are on Pinterest.

2) Following the boards of other random Pinterest users.

Pins are then *"Re-pinned"* and/or *"Liked"* by other *"Pinners"* and vice-versa.

Now with all of that having been said, some people (including regular users) still have no idea how to use Pinterest effectively. However, for most people this is irrelevant. For most people Pinterest is just a place to look at pretty things. In my opinion this isn't the worst thing in the world. However, if you do want to use it more strategically you must devise a plan. This plan should consist of the following 3 steps:

1) Strategically create boards that showcase your "Personal Brand Portfolio"

2) Strategically pin images and videos that best tell your "Personal Brand Story"

3) Strategically follow boards and pinners that Enhance your on-line "Personal Brand Network"

Showcasing Your Personal Brand Identity on Pinterest

Pinterest is an excellent way to display your professional portfolio and accomplishments. You can pin videos that you've created, covers of books that you've written or images of infographics and images that you've designed. You can pin them to Boards with straightforward names like "My Books" or give your boards eye-catching or thought-provoking names that showcase your creativity. Some examples of other ways that you can use Pinterest as a personal branding tool are as follows:

1) Create a shareable online **Brand Identity Package** by pinning images of your logo, business card, brochure, etc.

2) Create a shareable **On-line Resume**. (You might do this by sharing an image of each school that you've attended and job that you've had, along with explanatory text for each pin in the "Description" field)

3) Create boards that tell your unique **"Personal Brand Story"** (The potential ways to use Pinterest to do this are unlimited)

Adding Friends and Liking Boards

If you choose to use Pinterest solely for the purpose of building your personal brand, you may want to be more selective about the friends that you add and boards that you follow. If you're only adding pins and creating boards that tell your Personal Brand story, then you should try to be more selective than on other social networks. Much in the same way that you add connections on LinkedIn, you should try to share your pins with people that you are trying to build a professional relationship with.

The primary gateway for adding friends is via your existing FaceBook network. You already share images with those people on that platform. Therefore it would be more effective to select only some of these friends to be a part of your Pinterest network. It is worth mentioning that most people on Pinterest will just be sharing pictures of gourmet food, beautiful people and nice clothes. The good news is that you can still pin these images to the "Your Likes" page by clicking on the "Like" button found on each pin. So you can still participate in the social experience of Pinterest while working to promote and build your on-line Personal Brand Identity.

Happy Pinning! – To get started visit **www.Pinterest.com**

Using Visual Content to Enhance Your LinkedIn Profile

by **Vince Rogers**

When it comes to career and professional branding, **LinkedIn** *www.linkedin.com* is the most powerful tool available on the World Wide Web. It enables users to manage a well conceived and consistent on-line personal strategy. LinkedIn empowers them to control the dynamic content they share and the important people they share it with. Now LinkedIn has responded to the needs of savvy professionals who desire to add unique visual content to their profiles as well. This enables users to further distinguish themselves from their competition.

Standing out from the competition is the primary objective for achieving success with your branding strategy on LinkedIn. In the process of creating a powerful LinkedIn profile, most people simply strive for completeness and accuracy. They rely on effectively communicating their skills verbally. The only advantage comes from hopefully doing this better than the competition. Yet for a decision maker examining one after the other text heavy profiles, using the right words just may not be enough to grab their attention. Effective writing is certainly a powerful tool, but in many cases *Using Visual Content to Enhance Your LinkedIn Profile* may be the best way to gain a leg up on the competition.

Visual content includes (but is not limited to) the following:

1) *Videos*

2) *PowerPoint Presentations*

3) *Infographics*

4) *Book Covers*

Of course with any successful branding strategy, you must take time to conceive and execute a plan that will produce your desired outcome. This strategy should achieve the dual goal of positioning you as a trusted expert and networking with the people you want to make aware of your expertise.

There are essentially *4 Keys to Creating a Successful Branding Strategy on LinkedIn:*

1) *Upload a Profile Photo that tells your Brand Story in one image*

2) Complete your Powerful Profile page

3) *Strategically Build Your Network of Contacts.*

4) *Join the Right Groups.*

When you complete the major sections of your LinkedIn profile (*Summary, Experience and Education*) you will now find a new symbol next to the word *"Edit"*. This symbol is also found beneath the individual entries in each section. This button enables you to *"Click to add a video, image, document presentation…."* It also allows you to *"Add a Link"* or *"Upload a file"*.

Some tips to consider when uploading visual content you should consider are to:

1) *Only upload unique content that you have created*

2) *Only display your best work not the most work*

Brand conscious professionals are using visual content to enable visitors to see the product of their labor rather than just a simple description of their work. For example an Artist or Chef may want to share a picture of their most eye-catching creations. On the other hand, an Anchorman or Public Speaker would greatly benefit from uploading a video of them commanding an audience rather than simply state that they are a dynamic orator. Savvy professionals who use visual content effectively on LinkedIn will find it to be a "game changer" It is an essential tool for empowering their on-line branding strategy. Used effectively it will enhance your perceived expertise and the quality of the professional contacts that you attract.

Is Your Industry Dying or Changing?
by **Vince Rogers**

What comes to mind when you hear the words *book store, post office, home phone* or *public library*? These entities used to be as fundamental to our way of life as air and water. Now physical books are being replaced by e-readers, letters in your mailbox have been cancelled out by e-mails in your inbox and the mobile-phone has diminished the combined necessity of the precision wristwatch, the digital camera, the pocket calculator and even the portable music player. Technological advancement and consumer demand are acting in unison to interject constant change into all aspects of our lives'.

Some people say that all change is good. Yet, that doesn't change the fact that sometimes it catches many people completely off guard. If you are unprepared for change you can become overwhelmed, anxious and even downright desperate. Change often happens in gradual recognizable steps, rather than rapid surges. Nevertheless, most of us tend to have change thrust upon us instead of being prepared.

The changes that I've already mentioned affect people not just as consumers, but also affect your current and future career decisions. Staying on top of changes and trends in your industry must become a vital concern, regardless of whether you're a new-hire or a seasoned executive. In fact, knowing what's going on in your industry can make the difference between whether you're looking forward to receiving a big promotion or being abruptly laid off. A savvy, career-focused employee should put themselves in a position to recognize the signs well in advance.

For instance let's consider the future of the aforementioned public library. The internet has become most people's principle research tool. The internet and e-books have replaced the need to sift through the card catalog or lug home a big heavy book. Furthermore, the coffee shop has become the preferred destination of those who wish to eat, drink and be merry while they read. They prefer this more social setting to being constantly reminded by the mean old librarian to shush. Yet in Birmingham, England they just recently constructed a new $300 million (£188m) library!

So what do they know that we don't? Apparently, they know that regardless of changes in the future customers that they serve and the changing format of the product that they deliver; there is still a vital need for a free public space that educates people. The big question is determining what type of resources do they need to make available to their changing public? According to Brian Gambles, a project director at the new library in Birmingham, the library of the future must contribute to the surrounding community by actively being a *"....part of a better economic future...."* It can no longer just be a place to sit and read a good book.

This type of proactive approach to embracing and understanding change is not just limited to progressive Brits. Here in Atlanta at the West End Branch of the public library system, Robert E. White a Library Associate, is embracing the change he saw taking place in his industry and responding to the needs of the surrounding community. Over the years, the library has incorporated special programming that suits the specific needs of the patrons that they serve. They provide offerings that range from sewing classes that cater to the local Senior communities, to Search Engine Optimization workshops that target aspiring entrepreneurs hoping to join the ranks of thriving West End businesses.

White was inspired by personal vision and professional necessity to enter a Master's degree program in order to enhance his understanding of changes in his industry. He is now envisioning a plan to one day transform the library from a learning center into an empowerment institution. White believes that the Library will one day become a *"....Regional Center for continuing education and economic empowerment that fills in the learning gaps for all types of education, career and business development needs...."* This focus is indicative of the type of control and confidence that comes from having a proactive commitment to understanding the changes taking place in your industry.

In addition to earning a new advanced degree in your field like Mr. White, some other ways to keep up with changes in your industry are as follows:

1) Ask the Audience – Create a questionnaire or opinion poll that helps you gain information about how your industry is perceived by customers, co-workers, clients, etc.

2) Phone-a-Friend – Find an expert in your field or mentor that you can regularly communicate with about changes in your industry.

3) Final Answer – Once you have decided on a course of action, be decisive. Take action, whether it means looking for new opportunities in your current industry, or switching to a new career field altogether.

People often refer to the decline of the "Buggy Whip" industry, due to the emergence of the automobile, as a metaphor for companies being unresponsive to change. In actuality, few industries totally disappear. Yet all industries experience change and transformation. Understanding the changes taking place in your industry can be the key to building a career based on processing good information, instead being at the mercy of other people making moves.

You Need A Bio!
by **Vince Rogers**

Your resume is like a personal Operating Statement. Your Education section states what you've invested in your enterprise over time. Your Experience section shows the output that you have produced over time. Hopefully, when you present this statement to a potential prospect, it provides a clear picture of your overall career Net Worth.

It has probably been years since many of you have been asked for a resume. This is primarily because you have achieved a level of expertise and generated a word of mouth reputation that opens most doors. Yet at some point, you will ultimately be asked to produce a resume. This may be the case when pursuing some opportunity that requires verifiable documentation of credentials.

Yet in most cases, you will probably just be asked for a simple resume to document your professional accomplishments. If that is the case, you may make more of an impression by producing a compelling personal Bio instead. If your resume is a simple operating statement, then the Bio is a bottom line statement of the overall intrinsic and extrinsic value of your Personal Brand. A well written Bio differentiates you from the competition and positions you as an authority in your field.

Everybody loves a good story. More importantly, good personal or professional relationships are built upon people *connecting* with each other. There is probably no better way to get people to like you than to get them to connect with your story. Your resume enables a person to know something about you, but your bio compels them to get to know you.

One of the acknowledged experts on writing a Bio is Storytelling expert Michael Margolis the *"Dean"* of Story University **www.getstoried.com** According to Margolis, there are 3 questions all people want to know about you:

1. Do I share something in common with you?

2. How do we relate to each other?

3. Are you relevant to my success?

He insists that nowadays it's your Bio that people want to read first, not your resume. In order to make you Bio stand out, he claims that it must also answer the following 5 Questions:

1. Who am I?

2. How can I help you?

3. How did I get where I am?

4. Why can you trust me?

5. What do we share in common?

Personally, I have 4 different Bios for: Business; Leadership; Writing and Academics. While you may not need four bios (and I probably don't either) these are 4 good categories to consider when constructing your Bio. The goal is to turn your list of accomplishments into a compelling narrative. You may do this by answering the following 4 questions

1. Why did you choose the school you attended and your discipline or major?

2. Why did you become a published writer and why do you write about these subjects?

3. Why did you choose to take positions of leadership in your industry or community?

4. Why did you choose your profession and why do you want to continue in the future?

By answering these questions and following the steps outlined previously, you should be able to create a very compelling narrative. Undertaking the exercise of writing your Bio should also provide you with some clarity and perspective about your past, present and future professional goals. Being able to tell your story is an essential component to building your personal brand. Writing your Bio should also enable you to assess how effectively you are presenting your Personal Brand and help direct the course of your future Personal Strategy.

Of Mentors and Mastermind Groups
by **Vince Rogers**

Suppose that you were a novice investor, presented with two options for learning to understand the ins and outs of navigating the markets. The first option would be attending regularly scheduled face-to-face meetings with legendary investor Warren Buffet. The other choice presented to you is attending weekly group discussions between beginning, intermediate and experienced investors. Which alternative would you choose?

Warren Buffet is arguably the most successful investor in history. Most up-and-coming investors would probably consider regular interaction with him to be the ultimate choice. However, because of the resources that Mr. Buffet has at his disposal, his risk and reward decisions are based on buying thousands of shares of a stock. The deals that he might suggest to you may prove to be impractical if you can only buy just a few shares.

Conversely, the weekly meetings with a wide range of investors might provide you with exposure to variety of useful information. However, if you have recently inherited millions of dollars and just happen to have an MBA in Finance, you may benefit more from the weekly buffet with Buffet. A combination of both close intimate personal and dynamic group interactions might be the preferable way to obtain the career guidance you seek. Therefore, it is important that you understand how to choose the right trusted Mentor and/or how to join or form an effective Mastermind Group

Defining Mentors and Mastermind Groups

The term *Mentor* is of ancient origins. Mentor is a figure from Greek mythology who during the Trojan War was the advisor of Telemachus, the son of Odysseus. The modern mentor/mentee relationship can be formal or informal. The fundamental characteristic of the relationship is that a more experienced or knowledgeable person (Mentor) provides some form of guidance to another person (Mentee).

A *Mastermind Group* is a more recent conception. The idea derives from a term introduced by *Napoleon Hill* in the classic self-development book *"Think and Grow Rich"*. However, such advisory council type relationships have existed as long as human beings have formed organizations. Hill defined a Mastermind Group as follows: *"The coordination of knowledge and effort of two or more people, who work toward a definite purpose, in the spirit of harmony."*

The concept of the Mastermind Group had been out of fashion for a time. Yet with the advent of other collaborative business and professional tools such as *Social Networking, Coworking, and Crowdfunding* the use of collaborative tools and resources are now all the rage. Conversely, until lately the Mentor concept has been in vogue. Yet in recent years the mentoring model and the associated expectations of such relationships are now being regarded by some as outdated and unrealistic.

Finding a Mentor or a Mastermind Group.

As stated earlier, I don't think the choice is really an either or proposition. Mentoring relationships are valuable and successful ones are priceless. Mentoring relationships may come about organically through a chance meeting or via an introduction by a mutual friend. They may also be formal relationships such as apprenticeships or a condition for being accepted into a professional organization. To help you find an empowering mentoring relationship, here are a few suggestions that you might consider:

1. Clarity - Be clear about why you want a Mentor and your expectations from the relationship.

2. Compatibility - Your personality and communications styles should be conducive to developing a good working relationship.

3. Connection - A mentor should be someone who mirrors your own values, not just someone who has achieved the career stature that you'd like to achieve.

4. Collaboration – In all successful relationships, *reciprocity is the recipe for prosperity*. You should seek to contribute as much to the relationship as you expect to withdraw.

There are several different ways to find a Mastermind Group. For example, you can participate in your existing LinkedIn.com groups online or find face-to-face opportunities via Meetup.com. However, a very strategic way of finding the Mastermind Group that best suits you is to start it yourself. Some tips for starting a Mastermind Group are as follows:

1. Make a list of the ideal people that you would like to interact with, whether you know them or not.

2. Begin to invite them one by one to have coffee or a meal in an informal setting.

3. Then invite a few key people to an informal gathering at your home or other casual setting where you also discuss the formation of the Mastermind Group.

4. After gaining a commitment from your key people, and interest from other prospective members, arrange to have your first meeting.

Finding the right *Mentor* or joining the right *Mastermind Group* could lead to expanding your personal brand in ways that you couldn't imagine. A Mentor can help you to expand your vision and avoid common pitfalls on the road to success. Membership in a dynamic and diverse Mastermind Group can expand your career horizons exponentially. Gaining access to either one or both could prove to be the best career decisions that you ever make.

Developing a S.M.A.R.T. Career Plan

by **Vince Rogers**

Whether you are choosing a first career or changing careers, you need a career plan. After carefully assessing your *Skills and Talents* and defining your *Unique Selling Proposition*, you should now be ready to identify the industry and specific occupations that you are interested in. Finding the best career opportunity is the ultimate goal of your career plan. Personal development and goal setting experts have determined that the best way to achieve any goal is to be *S.M.A.R.T.* about it.

S.M.A.R.T. is an acronym for an achievement process that stands for *Specific, Measurable, Attainable, Relevant and Time-Bound*. The concept is derived from the pioneering work of management guru *Peter Drucker*. The idea is founded upon the belief that goals are more likely to be achieved if they are precisely defined. Rather than saying *I'm going to buy a new car*, an example of a S.M.A.R.T. goal would be *I am going to buy a 2014 Lexus LS Hybrid for less than $120,000 by December 3rd 2014*.

This goal of buying the Lexus is specific because it identifies an exact year, make and model of car. We can measure whether the goal is attained by whether I am able to acquire the vehicle below the specified price. By setting an exact date, I am challenging myself to follow the necessary plan that is required to achieve the goal. Yet when it comes to your career plan, there are a few additional considerations.

Specific

There may be some preliminary steps that you need to take on the road to obtaining your ultimate job. You might have to earn your Bachelor's degree first and start out as a kindergarten teacher's aide on the path to becoming a college professor. Nevertheless, you should seek to identify your ultimate career ambition rather than a short-term job objective. The various jobs and educational pursuits that lead to your ultimate goal should be considered as rungs on the ladder to ultimate career success.

Measurable

Attaining the position that you seek is not the only measurement of successfully reaching your career goal. While formulating your plan, you might consider the salary, work hours, and location of your ideal job. However, you should also think about less tangible aspects of a career such as stress level, professional integrity, and work-life balance. You should measure success by the overall satisfaction that you derive from your career, not just how much money you make.

Attainable

We are all at different stages in our lives and possess different competencies and capabilities. If you have properly researched your career alternatives, you should discover the industry and positions for which you are best suited. However, it may be difficult to resist the tendency to pursue a career for the wrong reasons. Pursuing a career that is not best suited to your personality, age, education, or ability is inadvisable.

Relevant

If you have carefully researched you career alternatives, hopefully your search has led you towards pursuing a career in a thriving industry. This may not always be possible given your educational attainment and transferable skills. As the economic landscape changes it is best to be involved in an industry where career prospects are growing. If you are not currently well suited to a viable industry, it might be worth the investment to pursue continuing education or internship opportunities that prepare you to make a career change.

Time-Bound

As stated earlier, setting a specific date forces you to follow the steps that are necessary to achieve your goal. The tendency to take some shortcuts should be avoided at all cost. However, while on the long road to becoming a doctor, you may find that you are better suited to be a Pharmacist. Nevertheless, if you find that you are indeed on the right career path, you should be committed to investing whatever time that it takes to reach your ultimate goal.

Getting S.M.A.R.T.E.R.

Now that you are on the S.M.A.R.T. road to achieving your career goals, you should make an immediate commitment to becoming even *S.M.A.R.T.E.R.* You must consistently *Evaluate* your plan to determinate if your career goal is still valid and viable. Then you must *Review* your plan regularly to make sure that you are always focused and on the right track.

Developing a *S.M.A.R.T.* career plan might sound like a lot of work. Yet without one, your career search might become aimless and stagnant. Taking the time to create *Specific, Measurable, Attainable, Relevant and Time-Bound* career goals may be the difference between becoming stuck in a dead end job or flourishing in a satisfying career. To insure that you stick to your plan, you must also commit to becoming even *S.M.A.R.T.E.R* by regularly *Evaluating* and *Reviewing* your plan.

Home of the Braves – Understanding Your Target Audience
by **Vince Rogers**

The Atlanta Braves are one of the most storied franchises in Major League Baseball. They rank #10 on the list of most World Series appearances with a total of 9. Nine, you might ask? Why I'm a loyal, lifelong, die-hard Braves fan and I only remember 5 appearances by Atlanta, you might say.

Well the fact of the matter is that the Braves are also the most mobile franchise in American professional baseball history. Despite the uproar over the recent announcement that the Atlanta Braves are moving to a new Cobb County, Georgia location by the start of the 2017 season, in the past the Braves have also called Boston and Milwaukee home. Yet this move within the same Metropolitan area is somewhat unprecedented. The shift in location is seemingly based solely on matters of branding, positioning and responsiveness to their target audience.

On November 11th, John Schuerholz the General Manager of the club announced that *"We are extremely excited that our address will still be Atlanta and so will the name across our jersey."* Despite this assurance that the team was not abandoning their allegiance to the name *"Atlanta"*, residents of the city proper – Atlanta, they regarded the team's announced move as an alienation of affections. The team's diverse fan-base of Black and White, affluent and working class and urban and suburban devotees had supported the team through more years of thin than thick. Now it seems that the only loyalty the team is being responsive to is the opportunity to move to *"greener pastures"*.

Schuerholz would go on to say in his video statement that *"We wanted to find a location that is great for our* fans, *makes getting to and from the stadium much easier, and provides a first-rate game day experience in and around the stadium."* These words left many people who felt that they were Braves *fans* scratching their heads. Well the fact of the matter is that what Mr. Schuerholz really meant was Target Audience – not fans. Yet in the GM's short statement, he captured all of the elements that should go into the hard realities of understanding your Target Audience.

Location

As evidenced by the above map of the Braves' 2012 season ticket purchasers, the heaviest concentration of paying fans live much closer to the proposed new stadium location than to the current one. The team further elucidates the question of access and location on their transition website **http://homeofthebraves.com/overview** They state that *"The reason for moving is simple…. our fans, access to Turner Field. There is a lack of consistent mass transportation, a lack of sufficient parking and a lack of direct access to interstates"*. Simply put, a business should try their best to be easily accessible to their target customer.

Ability to Pay

The aforementioned statement by the team mentions providing a first-rate game day experience as another reason for the move. The alternative translation is not based on what the audience demands, but based on what else can the team supply to a wealthier customer. According to *Wikipedia*, as of 2007, the median income was *$70,472* in Cobb County compared to *$45,171* in the City of Atlanta in 2010. By having better access to a more affluent fan-base, the team will be able to open up new profitable revenue streams, such as dining, merchandising and other ancillary income opportunities.

Psychographic Targeting

Psychographic Targeting is a fancy way of saying that you need to know what your customers like. One essential but touchy aspect of the Braves decision to move is that the game of baseball is not as attractive to non-White inner city residents as it used to be. In recent years initiatives have been taken to revive Black youths interest in the game. Nevertheless, interest in *"America's Favorite Pastime"* and the target audience's connection to the team better reflects the demographics of Cobb County.

As emotionally and economically disruptive as the Atlanta Braves decision to move the team to Cobb County may be for the City of Atlanta, as a business decision it is pretty sound. In your efforts to determine, understand and respond to the needs of your target audience, it would be wise to regard the same criteria as this beloved successful franchise. Access to your target customer, their ability to pay and their psychographic characteristics are inescapable considerations. Hopefully, the City of Atlanta will create new opportunities out of this situation, the Braves will find success in Cobb County and you will master the process of understanding your target audience as a means to building a major league brand.

<u>Take Note</u>

www.ingramcontent.com/pod-product-compliance
Lightning Source LLC
Chambersburg PA
CBHW022058170526
45157CB00004B/1390